Broken

Leona Mathew

BookLeaf Publishing

Presentation by *BookLeaf Publishing*

Web: www.bookleafpub.com

E-mail: info@bookleafpub.com

ISBN: 9789357211574

First edition 2023

DEDICATION

To Life

ACKNOWLEDGEMENT

I am really grateful to Bookleaf publishing, for the opportunity to finally put my thoughts out there. I used to struggle to make a start with this dream of mine to finally publish one article or poem that I have written in my moments of despair. The experience was really refreshing and I hope to see more opportunities as this come in life.

PREFACE

Writing always felt like a challenge to me and seeing other authors and even high school students write made me feel that I was not capable. But feelings that you harbour within yourself would always find a way to be expressed. I started writing poems just to express how I felt at certain moments in my life and to be honest the theme may seem very similar. But the fact that you can articulate those feels in different ways is amazing.

All of us need to express ourselves. Speak what's buried deep within ourselves.Hoping that this small book would allow you to see that we just need to express it. It brings you a lot of peace when you do.

I Am A Mistake

I am a mistake you never want to repeat,
A secret you will forever keep,
I am that person whom you will mistreat,
And one day regret for this deed.

Silly me, I fell head over heels,
What right did I have to appeal?
What's not mine can never be,
Especially to a worthless being like me.

Hand on my heart I want to thank you,
For the warmth you gave however minute,
For a bit this heart felt love again,
It has now learnt to refrain.

May happiness fill your life to come
May dreams come true every single one,
May love forever stay afresh,
And peace be with you till the end.

My Misconception

I am standing on the outside,
Longing to come in,
But this group is branded,
And I am from the bin

I am not one among you,
I thought I used to be,
My existence means nothing,
My misconception ; mistakably

I continue to look,
That's all I can do,
I thought you loved me,
I thought it was all true.

No-one Knows

I don't want to love anymore,
I wish I didn't fall,
I wish my mind had better control,
I wish I never met you at all.

The distance kept me happy,
The bitterness kept me sane,
The moment I let you in,
You unleashed all this pain.

At first I thought it was progress,
I gave this experiment another go,
But how wrong was I to believe,
I was worth anything anymore.

The sad part is you don't even know,
You are the reason for this aching,
What's worse is that I can't even share,
The horrible toll it is taking.

Each day I try to work on me,
To pick up the broken pieces,
But each time I gather myself up,
The burden in my heart increases.

It feels like a stab right through my heart,
bleeding me dry from inside,
No one knows what made me like this,
I sincerely wish I died

I am No one

I am no one
to anyone I knew
how foolish am I
for believing you

If I take a knife
and pierce myself
there is no one who cares
to call for help

My heart
Don't kid I have not one
For a heart belongs to a person
who knows how to love

I sit in solitude,
I search the darkness
I feel lifeless,
a rolling carcass

Your Life is Never Your Own

Your Life is never your own,
you are answerable to all,
even if you want to scream for help,
the answer is "its your fault."

Using ones culture as a weapon
how splendid the feeling is
not understanding due to ego
the downfall your character brings

How much more can one take
when stripped off everything sane
A slow venom taking over
making one numb to pain

I bid farewell to you all
I have nothing left to lose
this mind has closed forever
tradition prevails for good.

A Flickering Flame

A flickering flame
its been for years
eyes have dried
from all those tears

Then out of the blue
you walked in
turned this flame
into something

Initially this flame
struggled to thrive
but your tender care
brought this flame to life

Day after day
this flame grew
blazing with intensity
that this flame never knew

All was well
or so it seemed
the winds have changed
the elements deceived

This flame has promised
to burn for thee
never to cause..
melancholy

This flame shall never
get to be
the fire it wanted
you to see

It remains a flame
flickering by
slowly awaiting
for it to die.

Serendipity

I remember you sitting
right next to me
on that cold New Years eve
you sang the most melodious
song from the hymn
with a voice of
a canary
I remember looking
for this amazing being
that took my breath away
on sight
and my heart said
something it rarely says
my heart said
to this one hold on tight
I pity the other fools
who don't know what they overlooked
I am lucky they are not
so bright
Because I stumbled upon
a gem far for precious
and will hold her close
with all my might
she is delicate
though she has rough edges

she is strong
but very naive
she has the cutest smile
when she knows she's being foolish
and a scorching gaze
that could kill with ease
A woman like that
is hard to come across
and the fact that I have
shows that I am lucky
you have been an extraordinary friend
and I hope to be close by
and enjoy this
serendipity.

I Long to be Free

I long to be free
to live the truth
of who I am
and who I want to be

I long to be seen
not to utilised
for everyones needs

And then to be cast away
like I'm the only one
who made the big mistake.

Sometimes I wish I could escape
I wish these chains would break away
I wish I had the chance to fly away
and to never turn back to this pain.

Trust No one

I have a heart
in pieces they lie
I'm tired of picking them
I'm numb inside
I'll keep the pieces
but won't put them together
A high tower erected
the stronger the better
Never again will a mortal enter
Never again will you see me wither
I finally understood
That no-one can be trusted
I'm my own person
everyone else is corrupted.

Bitter Truth

When all is won or lost the same
only one person constantly remains
that one person is always yourself
no one else cares to offer help
Don't be upset it was always the case
from childhood till now the truth always stayed
in between hope got the better of you
atleast now you got a better view
People come just to help themselves
no one wonders if you've been through hell
they get what they want and bid farewell
leaving you exactly at the place you fell
I'm an asshole, a bitter hag
what else did you expect, fun chad?
this is what you made me become
it's too late for it to be undone.

Photograph

What do you see when you look through a lens?
Is it the beauty of the birds, the river the fence?
Or the simple pleasures of people just being
The truth in their eyes that's worth seeing.

Many actions that's we don't really observe
Captured in a motionless reserve
For many years down the line
To see and reminisce the passage of time

Things that were a sight to behold
Things that can't be seen anymore
Places mystical as the folks
Places that bring back lot of hope

Memories that evoke a lot of pain
Some of them with so less to gain
The colours also capture our eyes
Fills us up with delight

Of the many things I am yet to see
My camera always on my side shall be
To capture the moments I hold dear
To cherish for a lifetime of cheer.

Who am I?

Everyday I waste away
I try to be myself for me
I can't fully be who I am
As I am bound by societies expectations.

The clothes I wear,
The hair on my head
Even the person
Who sleeps in my bed

I moved away
For a sense of freedom
But I now realise
There is none

The more I close myself
To all
The more I become
Like a wall

No one really knows
The true me
I wonder if
If I know myself truly.

Is anyone themselves?

I am confused on who to please
the world at large or my inner being
I've been struggling with this since I can remember
Each time I kept telling myself it would get better

I see people who don't care at all
they do as they please and not as they are told
I do admire them for their decision
But I don't think I can go that distant.

Then there are people who live for others
some seem happy ,some are smothered
Again this kind of living makes me wonder
Could I be one of them down under?

All I know is I live in fear everyday
with a smile on my face like I'm okay
The truth is that I am definitely not
it doesn't matter though, cause no one asks.

NHS Abuse

Dear patients can you not just be
a little more considerate and live
why are you determined to to repeat the story
by making the same old folly?

You come in with issues, we try to sort
we give you medications that's worth a lot!
you come and go as you please
and disrespect the system with glee

This system was meant for people in need
not for people to misuse in greed
How in greed you might ask
when you take more than required, really that
sucks

There are countries who crave for such care
but you people are so unaware
How much you waste by taking things for
granted
you will only learn once left empty handed.

The staff are not your servants to sneer
or manhandle and instill fear
They too are humans just like you

choosing to work it through.

Be grateful for the life you have
Be cheerful for the system set
You predecessors had a dream
please don't make that less than it seems

Education

What is education?
is it teaching fact?
Or does it mean
to teach people how to act?

Schools of today
are all about competition
No one really cares
What the person has learnt in the end

What they have learnt
can it be used for good?
or is the knowledge
used as it should?

Everyone says education
begins at home
but do we give value
to that at all?

Learning to be mindful
is a basic thing
to the beginning of education
humanity and everything

Hoping we slowly move
back on to track
hoping education brings
humanity back

Journey

A path unknown
more or less
makes this journey
kind of a mess

Decisions we take
calculated or not
may not always
turn out as we thought

Some get lucky
they make it big
some get beaten down
until they are sick

sick of fighting
this battle called life
sick of being laughed at
by people filled with spite

But life always teaches
never to give up
it keeps going at us
till we are tough

Tough to make it
on our own
Tough to withstand
any man in this world

The destination
however sweet it may be
matters the most but
the journey is the key.

Music

A lyric mostly
makes a lot of sense
when you go through
something similar
The joy or pain
behind the penmanship
comes to life
in those instances
And when we are out
of that mindset
the lyrics once again
becomes obsolete
till the vicious circle
goes round again
and the emotional rollercoaster
repeats

Take a Chance

Taking a chance
on yourself
is always going
to be scary

When no one else believes
apart from yourself
may look like
you are daring

One thing to remember
its not them that matters
As people don't know
your demons

Keep trodding on
and remain strong
one day it all this
will make sense.

www.ingramcontent.com/pod-product-compliance
Lightning Source LLC
Chambersburg PA
CBHW051753130826
49812CB00033B/1139
* 9 7 8 9 3 5 7 2 1 1 5 7 4 *